Holidays

Celebrate
Thanksgiving

Deborah Heiligman
Consultant, Dr. Elizabeth Pleck

CHASE BRANCH LIBRARY
17731 W. SEVEN MILE RD.
DETROIT, MI 48235
578-8002

NOV 09

NATIONAL GEOGRAPHIC
WASHINGTON, D.C.

family

A Texas farmer and his son harvest soybeans.

turkey

In Autumn, when fields are full and crops are ready, people all over the world give thanks for the harvest.

In the United States, on the fourth Thursday in November, we celebrate Thanksgiving.

We celebrate with turkey, family, and counting blessings.

> *A wild turkey in Florida*

counting blessings

We hear about what

we call the "first Thanksgiving." In 1621, new English settlers in Plymouth, Massachusetts, celebrated a good harvest. They had survived a difficult year with the help of the Wampanoag Indians who lived there already.

The Wampanoag had been having festivals of thanks for many years. So when they heard the English celebrating, they killed five deer and brought them to the harvest festival to share.

∧ At a reenactment at Plimoth Plantation, English settlers welcome Wampanoag Indians to their celebration.

We hear about the "first Thanksgiving."

< A cornucopia of squash, vegetables, and nuts

> Felicity Duran performs Thanksgiving songs with her classmates in Hobbs, New Mexico.

They feasted on venison, roast duck, geese, clams, lobster, oysters, fish, Indian corn, dried berries, and stewed pumpkin. We don't know for sure if they ate wild turkey. We know they did not have cranberry sauce, potatoes, pumpkin pie, or apple pie. All of that came later.

For three days the 52 Pilgrims (as they came to be called) and 90 Indians played games and sports, sang, and danced. And they feasted!

< A Wampanoag feasts at Plimoth Plantation.

They feasted.

< A man throws two hatchets at the Thanksgiving Festival at Berkeley Plantation. The event marks the Thanksgiving day held in Virginia in 1619, which was actually the first Thanksgiving observed by English settlers in America.

v Dogs eat, too, at Plimoth.

The history of what happened between European settlers and Native Americans in our country is a sad one. In Plymouth, a few years after the feast there was a war between the settlers and the Indians. Many of the Wampanoag were killed. All over our country there were battles, and the Native Americans were forced from their land. Today some Indians mourn on Thanksgiving. Others feast on turkey and cranberry sauce with their families. Still others have special ceremonies of thanks, as they have done for thousands of years.

Some Indians mourn;

∧ *Andres Araica prays at the statue of Massasoit in Plymouth, Massachusetts, on the annual Day of Mourning, held on Thanksgiving.*

< Ashley Matt does a shawl dance during a Native American Thanksgiving meal served to elementary school children in Kalispell, Montana.

some have ceremonies of thanks.

> Every year the President of the United States grants an official pardon to a turkey, who is then allowed to live the rest of its life on a farm—instead of ending up as someone's Thanksgiving dinner.

After the feast in 1621,

Thanksgiving was not a regular celebration. We owe Thanksgiving as we know it today to a writer and editor named Sarah Josepha Hale. Sarah Josepha Hale thought all Americans should celebrate Thanksgiving day at the same time every year. She wrote to every President for more than twenty years. Finally, Abraham Lincoln declared a national day of Thanksgiving in 1863. Now every year we all celebrate on the same day.

> This is the Thanksgiving proclamation that President Lincoln issued on October 2, 1863. It created a national Thanksgiving holiday.

HAPPY THANKSGIVI

We all celebrate
on the same day.

We travel miles and miles.

Today, Thanksgiving is a true
national holiday. All over the United States,
we travel to celebrate with our families.
It is the biggest travel day of the year.
We travel miles and miles to be with our
grandparents, aunts, uncles, and cousins.
We drive, fly, take the train or the bus.

A father and daughter
arrive at the Los Angeles,
California, airport in time
for Thanksgiving.

We cook
and prepare.

v Members of a family in
   Seattle, Washington, check
   the Thanksgiving gravy.

For days we cook and prepare the dinner. On Thanksgiving day we cover our tables with a cornucopia of foods. We eat turkey with stuffing. We eat cranberry sauce, cornbread, and mashed potatoes. For dessert we have pies—pumpkin, sweet potato, apple, pecan.

∧ *Miriam Demaris takes a bite of pumpkin pie at her school Thanksgiving feast in Wheeling, West Virginia.*

> *Pumpkin, apple, and pecan pies baked for Thanksgiving.*

Some of our families have come from other countries. We add our own special flavors and foods to the feast. Most of us still have turkey, but when we make stuffing we use flavors and spices from our countries. And with our turkey we eat spring rolls, curry, black beans and rice, and pasta.

∧ *A woman prepares a Thanksgiving meal with Mexican flavor for new Latino immigrants in Los Angeles, California.*

< *In San Antonio, Texas, Rani Pemmaraju and Kalpana Rjagopal serve a Thanksgiving meal that includes traditional dishes from India.*

We add our own special flavors.

v *In Jacksonville, Florida, a family enjoys Thanksgiving dinner.*

We say a blessing.

For some of us, Thanksgiving is a religious day. Back in the time of the Pilgrims, there were harvest festivals and there were separate religious days of thanksgiving. Those days were solemn ones filled with prayer and fasting—not feasting. Today we combine the two. We pray at special services. Then we come home to feast! We say a blessing before our meal.

< *The Caedenas family prays after an interfaith Thanksgiving service in San Antonio, Texas.*

∧ In San Francisco, California, volunteers serve 7,000 Thanksgiving meals to homeless and poor people.

Thanksgiving is a time to

think of others who have less than we do. We invite people to share our Thanksgiving meals. We serve food at soup kitchens. We collect food for the poor. We share our bounty. We also feed our soldiers who are fighting in wars away from home.

> *Marie Schmidgall serves
Thanksgiving meals to
Verlee Millspaugh and
Mabel Pearsall at the annual
Community Thanksgiving
Dinner in Burlington, Iowa.*

We share our bounty.

< *Petty Officer 3rd Class
James Vanderlois (left)
and Seaman Eduardo
Rivera celebrate
Thanksgiving while
serving in the Iraq war.*

> *Many parades have marching bands. This is a b-flat tuba.*

We have other Thanksgiving traditions. We watch parades. Parades have been part of Thanksgiving since the 1800s. In New York City, the Macy's Thanksgiving Day Parade marks the day with marching bands, floats, and huge, fun balloons.

v *Emily Kinder and her cousin James Abla play football after their Thanksgiving feast in Salina, Kansas.*

We also watch football. All over the country, sports fans celebrate by playing and watching football. The tradition of playing sports comes from old harvest festivals, like the one in Plymouth in 1621.

We watch parades and football.

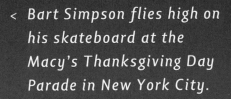

< *Bart Simpson flies high on his skateboard at the Macy's Thanksgiving Day Parade in New York City.*

At the end of

Thanksgiving day we feel full. We feel full of thanks, we feel full of family, we feel full of blessings. And we feel full of food!

We feel full!

> *In Burlington, Iowa, Kaviyaah Morgan offers his friend Lakendra Applegate his pumpkin pie at their school Thanksgiving meal.*

MORE ABOUT THANKSGIVING

Contents

Just the Facts

WHO CELEBRATES IT: Americans. (Canadians celebrate their own Thanksgiving at a different time.)

WHAT: A holiday to give thanks for our blessings; a day to remember the history of Native Americans.

WHEN: In the U.S., the fourth Thursday in November. (In Canada, the second Monday in October.)

RITUALS: Eating a big meal with turkey as the main dish; being with family; saying thanks.

TRADITIONS: Giving to the needy; watching and playing football; watching parades; praying.

FOOD: Turkey with stuffing is the traditional main dish. Also: cranberry sauce, cornbread, mashed potatoes, pumpkin pie, apple pie, and other regional and cultural foods.

Native American Thanksgiving Prayer

There are many prayers of Thanksgiving. This one is from the Iroquois.

We return thanks to our mother,
the earth, which sustains us.

We return thanks to the rivers and streams,
which supply us with water.

We return thanks to all herbs,
which furnish medicines
for the cure of our diseases.

We return thanks to the moon and stars,
which have given to us their light
when the sun was gone.

We return thanks to the sun,
that has looked upon the earth
with a beneficent eye.

Lastly, we return thanks to the Great Spirit,
in Whom is embodied all goodness,
and Who directs all things
for the good of Her children.

Timeline of American Thanksgiving

BEFORE 1620: Native People have lived in the area now called New England for more than 10,000 years. They fish, hunt, and grow crops. Like Native People all over America, they give thanks every day. They also hold harvest festivals.

DECEMBER 4, 1619: The first Thanksgiving in America by European settlers is held in Virginia on the James River. It is a day of prayer.

EARLY AUTUMN, 1621: Settlers in Plymouth, Massachusetts, hold a three-day harvest festival modeled after English "harvest home" festivals.

1622-1863: Feasts of thanksgiving and religious days of thanks held at different times.

1789: President George Washington proclaims November 26 a day of National Thanksgiving. The holiday does not stick.

1837: Sarah Josepha Hale starts campaigning for one National Thanksgiving celebration.

OCTOBER 3, 1863: President Lincoln declares a National Thanksgiving for the last Thursday in November. It remains so for 75 years.

1860s AND 70s: Baseball and football games are played on Thanksgiving day.

1871: *Harper's Weekly Magazine* runs a feature on turkey production and calls the turkey "Our Thanksgiving Bird." This is after years of campaigning by poultry producers to make turkey the main dish at Thanksgiving.

LATE 1800s: The people who came to Plymouth in 1620, now called the Pilgrims, become known as the first settlers, although they were not the first Europeans to settle America. People start talking about the "first Thanksgiving."

1924: Macy's Thanksgiving Day Parade is held for the first time.

1934: First National League Football Thanksgiving Day game is played.

1939: President Franklin D. Roosevelt sets Thanksgiving one week earlier to help the economy by lengthening the Christmas shopping season. This lasts for three years.

1941 TO PRESENT: Thanksgiving is celebrated the fourth Thursday of November. Each year the President issues a Thanksgiving proclamation.

1970 TO PRESENT: Some Native Americans gather at the statue of Massasoit, the Wampanoag leader, in Plymouth, Massachusetts, on Thanksgiving Day. They remember the struggles of their ancestors and honor the strength of the Wampanoag.

PhilPa's Cranberry & Peach Preserves

This delicious recipe is from Philip Goldsmith, the author's brother. (Be sure to have an adult help you at the stove.)

INGREDIENTS:

1 cup sugar

1 cup water

1 12-ounce package frozen cranberries

8 ounces canned sliced peaches, drained and cut into 1/2 inch pieces (about 2 cups)

1. Stir the sugar and water in a heavy medium saucepan over high heat until the sugar dissolves and the syrup comes to a boil.

2. Add the cranberries; return the mixture to a boil.

3. Reduce heat to medium: simmer until the cranberries burst and the sauce thickens slightly (about 10 minutes).

4. Remove from heat. Let stand for five minutes.

5. Mix in peaches. Cool.

6. Chill at least two hours. Then enjoy with your turkey!

Harvest Festivals Around the World

For thousands of years people all over the world have held special festivals to give thanks for a good harvest. American and Canadian Thanksgivings were modeled partly on the centuries-old English "harvest home" tradition, a merry feast held after the last of the grain is brought in from the fields. The ancient Hebrew harvest festival called Sukkot is still celebrated every autumn by Jews around the world. Kwanzaa, observed by many African Americans, is based on age-old African harvest festivals.

Across the globe people celebrate their most important or favorite crop. In Switzerland they give thanks for onions. In France they celebrate the grape. Throughout Asia there are rice festivals. In Ghana there is a yam festival, and in Barbados a sugar cane festival. For which food would you like to give thanks?

∧ Dancers at a harvest festival in Kerala, India.

Find Out More

BOOKS

The books with stars (*) are appropriate for children.

*Anderson, Laurie Halse. *Thank You, Sarah: The Woman Who Saved Thanksgiving.* Simon & Schuster Books for Young Readers, 2002. This book brings Sarah Joseph Hale and her story to life.

Dennis, Matthew. *Red, White, and Blue Letter Days: An American Calendar.* Cornell University Press, 2002. Chapter 2 gives a detailed history and commentary on Thanksgiving from 1621 to 2000.

*Grace, Catherine O'Neill and Margaret M. Bruchac with Plimoth Plantation. *1621: A New Look at Thanksgiving.* National Geographic, 2001. A beautiful and historically sound book.

*Osborne, Mary Pope and Natalie Pope Boyce. *Pilgrims: A Nonfiction Companion to Thanksgiving on Thursday.* Random House, 2005. An interesting book of facts.

Pleck, Elizabeth H. *Celebrating the Family: Ethnicity, Consumer Culture, and Family Rituals.* Harvard University Press, 2000. Chapter 2, along with an encyclopedia entry written by Professor Pleck, guided my research for this book.

Siskind, Janet. "The Invention of Thanksgiving: A Ritual of American Nationality," in *Food in the USA: A Reader.* Edited by Carole M. Counihan. Routledge, 2002. Includes how settlers took advantage of Native Americans.

*Swamp, Chief Jake. *Giving Thanks: A Native American Good Morning Message.* Lee & Low, 1995. A beautifully written and illustrated thanksgiving prayer of the Six Nations people.

WEB SITES

http://www.plimoth.org
This site, put out by Plimoth Plantation living history museum, is a great resource.

http://www.pilgrimhall.org/daymourn.htm
A page about the National Day of Mourning in Plymouth.

http://www.bostonkids.org/educators/wampanoag/index.htm
A site for teachers about the Wampanoag.

http://www.macys.com/campaign/parade/parade.jsp
A fun Web site all about the Macy's Thanksgiving Day Parade.

Glossary

Cornucopia: a lot of something (more than you need). A container shaped like a goat's horn overflowing with fruits, vegetables, flowers, etc. to symbolize plenty. Also called "horn of plenty."

Editor: someone who helps get a book, magazine, or newspaper ready to be published.

Harvest: the crops that have ripened and are gathered; the process of gathering the crops.

Mourning: the feeling or showing of deep sadness after a loss.

Pilgrim: one of the English settlers who founded Plymouth colony. The word pilgrim is also used to mean a person who goes on a long journey or a person who makes a journey for religious reasons.

Venison: the meat of a deer, eaten as food.

Wampanoag (WAHM-puh-nog): Native Americans who lived (and still live) in the area that is now Eastern Massachusetts and Rhode Island. The name means "People of the First Light."

Where This Book's Photos Were Taken

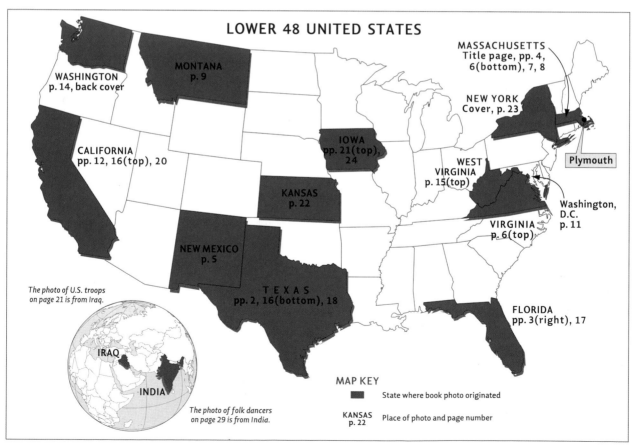

LOWER 48 UNITED STATES

MASSACHUSETTS
Title page, pp. 4, 6(bottom), 7, 8

NEW YORK
Cover, p. 23

WASHINGTON
p. 14, back cover

MONTANA
p. 9

CALIFORNIA
pp. 12, 16(top), 20

IOWA
pp. 21(top), 24

WEST VIRGINIA
p. 15(top)

Plymouth

Washington, D.C.
p. 11

KANSAS
p. 22

VIRGINIA
p. 6(top)

NEW MEXICO
p. 5

T E X A S
pp. 2, 16(bottom), 18

FLORIDA
pp. 3(right), 17

The photo of U.S. troops on page 21 is from Iraq.

IRAQ

INDIA

The photo of folk dancers on page 29 is from India.

MAP KEY

State where book photo originated

KANSAS
p. 22   Place of photo and page number

30

Thanksgiving: Its Meanings and Traditions

by Dr. Elizabeth Pleck

Thanksgiving, a much beloved American holiday, has had many meanings, beginning with a religious or spiritual one. For centuries people in many parts of the world devoted a special day to giving thanks to God for surviving hardship.

The holiday also has secular beginnings—in celebrating a good harvest. During the autumn of 1621, settlers in the English colony of Plymouth (now Massachusetts) were grateful. Even though they had had a severe winter during which many of their number had died, they had successfully planted a crop and harvested it. So they feasted and invited their Wampanoag neighbors (who outnumbered them). The event resembled the English "harvest home" custom, a somewhat raucous, entirely secular harvest festival.

The harvest festival of 1621 was never intended to be an annual event. Instead, after 1621 New England settlers generally observed days of thanksgiving in two separate ways. One was to spend a day in fasting and prayer, giving thanks for winning a battle or surviving a catastrophe such as a drought. The other was to have a big feast. In time these two ideas about thanksgiving merged into a single day, often celebrated in New England, but rarely in other parts of the country.

The idea of Thanksgiving as a day of family reunion appeared in the first half of the nineteenth century. Adult children were urged to visit their elderly parents to enjoy a special home-cooked feast during the autumn.

Sarah Josepha Hale was the single most important champion of the national day of Thanksgiving. Best known as the author of the nursery rhyme, "Mary's [Little] Lamb," Hale was the editor of a popular journal for women. She wrote to six presidents encouraging them to proclaim Thanksgiving as a national holiday. Southern nationalists prior to the Civil War were opposed to her idea because they associated Thanksgiving with antislavery sermons delivered in Northern churches on the day. Hale countered by presenting Thanksgiving as a means of preventing a civil war by celebrating shared American values.

During the Civil War, the victory at Gettysburg (as well as Hale's entreaties) encouraged President Lincoln to declare a national day of Thanksgiving in 1863. He asked all Americans to remember the widows and orphans of the Civil War, and he called upon God to help restore the divided country to one nation.

Over the years, more traditions have become associated with the holiday. The Thanksgiving Day football game began in the 1870s as the culminating contest in the Ivy League football season. In the Progressive era, Thanksgiving became a holiday that incorporated immigrants into American customs.

The National Day of Mourning began in 1970 as a Wampanoag speaker criticized the myth of entirely friendly relations between his people and the English settlers in Plymouth. It remains a day of protest as well as celebration of Native American traditions.

Of all the different meanings of Thanksgiving, the one that has best endured from Hale's day is the notion of the holiday as a time to go home to family. Every year on the fourth Thursday in November, people all over America gather with their loved ones to feast and give thanks.

Elizabeth A. Pleck

Elizabeth Pleck is Professor of History at the University of Illinois at Urbana-Champaign and the author of Celebrating the Family: Ethnicity, Consumer Culture, and Family Rituals.

For Henry Miller Brotman, born November 20, 2005

PICTURE CREDITS

Pages 1, 4 (top), 6 (bottom), 7: © Sissie Brimberg and Cotton Coulson; Page 2-3: © Scott Sinklier/ Corbis; Page 3(right): © Joe McDonald/Corbis; Page 4 (bottom): © Photodisc/Getty Images; Page 5: © Kimberly Ryan/ The News Sun/ Associated Press; Page 6 (top): © Mark Gormus/ Richmond Times Dispatch/ Associated Press; Page 8: © Neal Hamberg/ Associated Press; Page 9 © Robik Loznak/ Daily Inter Lake/ Associated Press; Page 10: Library of Congress; Page 11: © Trippett/SIPA Press; Page 12-13: © David McNew/ Getty Images; Page 14, 15 (bottom): © Ryan McVay/ Getty Images; Page 15 (top): © Scott McCloskey/ The Wheeling Intelligencer/ Associated Press; page 16 (top): ©Armondo Arorizo/ ZUMA Press; Page 16 (bottom): © BM Sobhani/ San Antonio Express/ ZUMA Press; Page 17: © Kwame Zikomo/ SuperStock; Page 18-19: © Nicol Fruge/ San Antonio Express/ ZUMA Press; Page 20: ©Julie Jacobson/ Associated Press; Page 21 (top), 24-25: ©John Lovretta/ The Hawk Eye/ Associated Press; Page 21 (bottom): ©SSgt. Demetrio J. Espinosa/ DOD/ ZUMA Press; 22 (top): © Photodisc/Getty Images; Page 22 (bottom): © Ryan Soderlin/ Salina Journal/ Associates Press; Page 23: © Joseph Sohm/ Corbis; Page 27: University of Texas; page 28: © Lori Epstein; page 29: © Dipak/Reuters/Corbis; Front cover: © Bernd Obermann/ Corbis; Back cover: © Ryan McVay/ Getty Images; Spine: © Chris Stephens/ The Plain Dealer/ Associated Press.

First paperback edition 2008
Text copyright © 2006 Deborah Heiligman
Composite copyright © 2006 National Geographic Society.
Published by the National Geographic Society.

All rights reserved. Reproduction of the whole or any part of the contents without written permission from the National Geographic Society is strictly prohibited. For information about special discounts for bulk purchases, contact National Geographic Special Sales: ngspecsales@ngs.org.

Library of Congress Cataloging-in-Publication Data
Heiligman, Deborah.
  Celebrate Thanksgiving / Deborah Heiligman ; consultant, Elizabeth Pleck.
    p. cm. — (Holidays around the world)
  ISBN 0-7922-5928-9 (hardcover) — ISBN 0-7922-5929-7 (lib. bdg.)
  1. Thanksgiving Day—Juvenile literature. 2. Thanksgiving Day—History—Juvenile literature. I. Pleck, Elizabeth Hafkin. II. Title. III. Series: Holidays around the world (National Geographic Society (U.S.))
  GT4975.H44 2006   394.2649—dc22   2006008685
ISBN: 978-0-7922-5928-2 (trade hardcover)
ISBN: 978-0-7922-5929-9 (reinforced library edition)
ISBN: 978-1-4263-0292-3 (paperback)

Book design is by 3+Co.
The body text is set in Mrs. Eaves. The display text is in Lisboa.

FRONT COVER: At the 2003 Macy's Thanksgiving Parade in New York City, a giant inflated turkey promenades down Central Park West. BACK COVER: A girl watches as a nattily dressed young fellow gets ready to stick his finger into a pumpkin pie. TITLE PAGE: A boy enjoys the Thanksgiving feast during a reenactment at Plimoth Plantation.

One of the world's largest nonprofit scientific and educational organizations, the National Geographic Society was founded in 1888 "for the increase and diffusion of geographic knowledge." Fulfilling this mission, the Society educates and inspires millions every day through its magazines, books, television programs, videos, maps and atlases, research grants, the National Geographic Bee, teacher workshops, and innovative classroom materials. The Society is supported through membership dues, charitable gifts, and income from the sale of its educational products. This support is vital to National Geographic's mission to increase global understanding and promote conservation of our planet through exploration, research, and education.

For more information, please call 1-800-NGS-LINE (647-5463) or write to the following address:
NATIONAL GEOGRAPHIC SOCIETY
1145 17th Street N.W., Washington, D.C. 20036-4688 U.S.A.
Visit the Society's Web site at www.nationalgeographic.com

John M. Fahey, Jr., *President and Chief Executive Officer*
Gilbert M. Grosvenor, *Chairman of the Board*
Nina D. Hoffman, *Executive Vice President,*
  President of Books and Education Publishing Group
Stephen Mico, *Executive Vice President,*
  Children's Books and Education Publishing Group
Bea Jackson, *Design Director, Children's Books and Education Publishing Group*
Margaret Sidlosky, *Illustrations Director, Children's Books and Education Publishing Group*

STAFF FOR THIS BOOK

Nancy Laties Feresten, *Vice President, Editor-in-Chief of Children's Books*
Jennifer Emmett, Sue Macy, Marfé Ferguson Delano, *Project Editors*
Jim Hiscott, *Art Director*
Lori Epstein, *Illustrations Editor*
Carl Mehler, *Director of Maps*
Priyanka Lamichhane, *Editorial Assistant*
Rebecca Hinds, *Managing Editor*
R. Gary Colbert, *Production Director*
Lewis R. Bassford, *Production Manager*
Vincent P. Ryan, Maryclare Tracy, *Manufacturing Managers*

ACKNOWLEDGMENTS

For research help, many thanks to: Lari Robling, author of *Endangered Recipes: Too Good to Be Forgotten*; Valerie Vargas, who shared the Native American prayer with me; Benjamin Weiner, even though his research didn't make the final book; and Laurie Anderson, for a very helpful phone call. Thanks to the good people at the Bank Street Bookstore, who always have the right books. Thanks to Phil and Essie Goldsmith for always hosting wonderful Thanksgivings, and to my whole family for making them warm and fun. A grateful grin to the November 26 birthdays—Jon and Aaron—and to Mom, whose spirit still presides over the day. A special thanks to Laurie Miller Brotman (CL), whose timing made me finish my first draft.